A gift from **WALTON COMMUNITIES**
APAR

2181

Marietta, Georgia 3000

Phone: 678-303-4100

www.waltoncommunities.com

Our Mission Statement

We are committed to serving the needs of families with excellence through
the development and ownership of apartment communities.

CELEBRATING CHRISTMAS
EVERY DAY

CELEBRATING CHRISTMAS
EVERY DAY

*A Keepsake Devotional Featuring the
Inspirational Poetry of Helen Steiner Rice*

BARBOUR
PUBLISHING

CONTENTS

INTRODUCTION

*C*hristmas is more than a special day or special season. It's the time we have set aside to celebrate all that is precious to us: our families, our friends, our blessings, and of course, Jesus, whose birth is the substance and inspiration that carries us through our days.

All year long we save up our worship, our hopes, our dreams, our money, our family traditions, our favorite recipes, and our fondest memories all in anticipation of this grand holiday. Then we bring everything out at once in a frenzy of excited and joyful activities. We carefully set up the tree and hang the ornaments. We choose gifts for those we love. We send warm wishes and Christmas prayers to the people who have touched our lives in special ways. We interact with our neighbors and show appreciation to those who lighten our loads. We call our families together. We read the glorious story of Christ's birth and sing commemorative carols. We raise our voices in praise and worship to God for His Son, who brought light to our darkened world and quenched our thirsty hearts.

However, as wonderful as all this celebration may be, it's an awful lot to pack into a single day, week, or month. Try to imagine what the world would be like if Christmas became a constant in our lives and harmony, generosity, kindness, tolerance, love, joy, and peace reigned year-round. Perhaps we should make the grandest holiday of the year, the grandest holiday *throughout* the year. Perhaps we should celebrate Christmas all year long—one day at a time, one hour at a time, and one moment at a time.

THE PRICELESS GIFT OF CHRISTMAS

*N*ow Christmas is a season
    for joy and merrymaking,
A time for gifts and presents,
    for giving and for taking;
A festive, friendly, happy time
    with shoppers on their way—
But have we really felt
    the greatness of the day?
For through the centuries the world
    has wandered far away
From the beauty and the meaning
    of the Holy Christmas Day.
For Christmas is a heavenly gift
    that only God can give.
It's ours just for the asking
    for as long as we shall live.
It can't be bought or bartered,
    it can't be won or sold,
It doesn't cost a penny,
    and it's worth far more than gold.
It isn't bright and gleaming
    for eager eyes to see,
It can't be wrapped in tinsel
    or placed beneath a tree,

It isn't soft and shimmering
    for reaching hands to touch,
Or some expensive luxury
    you've wanted very much.
For the Priceless Gift of Christmas
    is meant just for the heart,
And we receive it only when
    we become a part
Of the Kingdom and the Glory
    which is ours to freely take,
For God sent the Holy Christ Child
    at Christmas for our sake
So man might come to know Him
    and feel His presence near,
And see the many miracles
    performed while He was here.
And this Priceless Gift of Christmas
    is within the reach of all:
The rich, the poor, the young and old,
    the greatest and the small.
So take His Priceless Gift of Love,
    reach out and you'll receive,
And the only payment that God asks
    is just that you believe.

~HSR

CELEBRATING FAMILY

LOVE SHARED

It is sharing and caring,
giving and forgiving,
loving and being loved,
walking hand in hand,
talking heart to heart,
seeing through each other's eyes,
laughing together,
weeping together,
praying together,
and always trusting and believing
and thanking God for each other. . .
For love that is shared is a beautiful thing—
It enriches the soul and makes the heart sing.

~HSR

Bound by Love

While they were there, the time came for the baby to be born,
and she gave birth to her firstborn, a son.
Luke 2:6–7

We live in a great big world—a world so overwhelming that it's sometimes easy to get lost. That's why God didn't leave us to drift alone through life. He grouped us into families and tied us together with love. What a wonderful gift!

At no other time of year are God's intentions for families more beautifully revealed than at Christmas. The Bible's account of the first Christmas is the story of a small family struggling to reach Bethlehem—their long and arduous journey made bearable only by their love and compassion for each other. Then, while still far from home, their first child is born in a borrowed stable, and the three of them huddle together for warmth. Can you imagine Joseph's strong, gentle hands—the hands of a master carpenter—comforting Mary as she labors to bring Jesus into the world? Can you see Mary gently stroking the face of her newborn as she and Joseph swaddle him and lay Him on His bed of hay? Shared love is what brings us through the best and worst of times. It is our beacon of hope on life's turbulent seas. Thank God this Christmas for the constant love of family.

TOGETHER

And where the home is filled with love
You'll always find God spoken of,
And when a family prays together,
That family also stays together.

~HSR

Joyous Reunion

How great is the love the Father has
lavished on us, that we should be called
children of God! And that is what we are!
1 John 3:1

No matter how humble the family
home, almost every soul yearns to return there on Christmas
morning. We are willing to sacrifice money and convenience just
to sit around that familiar tree with those we love. Those who
wait for us have longing hearts, too, counting down the hours
and minutes until we arrive. Everything is about preparation up
until that point, and only when everyone has gathered can the
celebration begin.

The joy and excitement that overwhelms us as we anticipate
being with our loved ones at Christmas is a picture of how
God waits and longs for us at all times. Imagine what it will be
like when all His children have gathered together. It will be a
celebration like no other we have ever known!

Is God still waiting for you to come home to His family? Don't
worry, He won't push or prod or trick you into coming. He will
simply wait, His heart bursting with love. He wants you to come
when you are ready, when your heart is longing to be there as
well—when something inside you knows that *His* family is *your*
family. Don't be late for the celebration!

PEACE

In seeking peace for all people
there is only one place to begin
And that is in each home and heart—
for the fortress of peace is within.

~*HSR*

FINDING REFUGE

To us a child is born, to us a son is given, and the government
will be on his shoulders. And he will be called Wonderful Counselor,
Mighty God, Everlasting Father, Prince of Peace.

ISAIAH 9:6

*P*eace is something we talk and sing about quite a bit at
Christmastime, but it is something rarely seen in the hectic
crunch of holiday cooking, shopping, decorating, and
entertaining. Financial anxiety often drowns out the angel's
message of "peace on earth, good will to men," and a mountain
of appointments and activities take the place of quiet intro-
spection and worship.

But it doesn't have to be that way. You can ask God to
establish His peace within you. Others will see it—in your
demeanor, in your countenance, in your words—and follow your
example.

You see, Jesus was not merely sent to bring peace to the
nations. His primary mission was to bring peace to the hearts of
men and women like us. We were estranged from our Father and
out of touch with our Creator until His entrance into the world
provided a cure for sin and its ravages. He made us right with
our God.

If you are seeking peace this Christmas, ask God to fill your
heart and mind until you feel calm on the inside. Then
ask Him to let your peace overflow into your
home and family. You can be sure it will.

LOVE IS THE LANGUAGE

Love is the language
that every heart speaks,
For love is the one thing
that every heart seeks. . . .
And where there is love
God, too, will abide
And bless the family
residing inside.

~HSR

SHOWER OF BLESSINGS

*Live a life of love, just as Christ loved us and gave himself
up for us as a fragrant offering and sacrifice to God.*
EPHESIANS 5:2

A lot of love gets passed around at Christmas. Those three little
words, "I love you," rarely spoken in some families, come easier
during the holidays. Gifts are exchanged and acts of kindness
abound. Everywhere we look is another message of love.

For many though, these messages can seem hollow and
lifeless. Whether it's due to poor choices, estrangements, or just
unfortunate circumstances, some individuals see Christmas as a
painful reminder of what is missing from their lives. But if they
could just look past their problems and disappointments, they
would see a God who is eager to introduce them to real love—a
love that is rich and full and will last forever.

Is your heart longing for love this Christmas? Perhaps
you have been born into a family that simply doesn't
have the capacity to be all you need them to be. Look to
God. He will never disappoint you or fall short of your
expectations. He loved you even before you were
conceived—before you had substance of any kind—and
He loves you still. He is right there waiting for you to
accept all that He has for you.

MEMORIES BRIGHTEN DARK DAYS

*T*ender little memories
    of some word or deed
Give us strength and courage
    when we are in need.
Blessed little memories
    help to bear the cross
And soften all the bitterness
    of failure and of loss.
Precious little memories
    of little things
      we've done
Make the very darkest day
    a bright and happy one.

~HSR

HEARTFELT TRADITIONS

We are bound to give thanks to God always for
you, brethren beloved by the Lord.
2 THESSALONIANS 2:13 NKJV

*O*ne of the primary tasks of family is to
preserve and pass down memories. It is
through this tradition that we often learn who we are and what
is expected of us. These family memories cover us, keep us, and
help us form positive attitudes about ourselves and the world.

As families gather and excitement fills the air, Christmas is
the perfect opportunity to make memories together. It is an ideal
time to instill the importance of family in the minds and hearts
of our children—the importance of our earthly family and God's
family, too.

Make lots of memories this Christmas. Don't get distracted
by those things that the world finds more important—especially
the empty hype of commercialism. Instead, make the holidays a
time to do things together, like read the Christmas story, act out
the nativity, and sing carols. That is the stuff lasting memories are
made of. These are the memories that will warm you when your
family ties are tested and the cold winds of adversity blow.

God has given us good times to get through the bad times, so
store up all the memories you can this Christmas by celebrating
and giving thanks for each member of your family.

THOUGHTS OF YOU

In my eyes there lies no vision
    but the sight of your dear face.
In my heart there is no feeling
    but the warmth of your embrace.
In my mind there are no thoughts
    but the thoughts of you, my dear.
In my soul, no other longing
    but just to have you near.
All my dreams were built around you,
    and I've come to know it's true:
In my life there is no living
    that is not part of you.

~HSR

In His Keeping

*A father of the fatherless, a defender of widows, is God in His holy
habitation. God sets the solitary in families.*
PSALM 68:5–6 NKJV

In Genesis, the very first book of the Bible, God says that it isn't
good for man to dwell alone. Even though Adam was blessed by
the company of his Creator, he needed someone like himself.
And so, God created woman, thereby blessing and establishing
the first family unit.

God says family is important, and for that reason alone we
should honor it at Christmastime and every other time of year.
Sometimes that requires dealing with situations we would
prefer to ignore and people we would prefer to forget. Perhaps
yours is an especially difficult family. Ask God to help you see
the good in each family member and preserve the ties that bind
you together when that is possible.

If your family is too badly broken and toxic, you have all
the more reason to ask God for His powers of forgiveness and
understanding. For others, there might not be a family nearby for
them to turn to as a result of thinning generations.

If you find yourself with a family this Christmas, you have
reason to celebrate. But if you do not, ask God to provide you
with a surrogate family. He will bring others around you—
perhaps others who are also seeking closeness and comfort. In
God's plan, no one is left out at Christmas or any other time of
the year.

TREASURED MEMORIES

*M*emories to treasure
are made every day—
Made of family gatherings
and children as they play.

~HSR

CHILDLIKE WONDER

[Jesus] said, "Truly I tell you, unless you change and become like children,
you will never enter the kingdom of heaven."
MATTHEW 18:3 NRSV

*I*t is and always has been magical to be a child at Christmas.
When we reach adulthood though, we tend to live vicariously
through the children around us, whether they are nieces,
nephews, grandchildren, or our own children. Their innocent
sense of expectation, mystery, and wonder is contagious—if
just for a little while. Though our perspectives change as adults,
it is a truly good thing to feel hope and wonderment in our
hearts. After all, the Bible tells us these qualities are essential for
entering the kingdom of heaven.

We quickly become jaded by the holidays as our list of
responsibilities and things to do gets longer every year. We
begin to approach our lives and activities with caution, putting
the things of childhood behind us.

God doesn't want us to act childishly, but He does
want us to be childlike in regard to our relationship
with Him. It is the one aspect of our lives in which we
are allowed to identify ourselves as children—
His children. God is delighted when we come to Him
with childlike faith, stand in awe of His greatness,
and wait expectantly for His answers.

This Christmas, tell your heavenly Father what
you would like to receive from Him. Just close your
eyes and speak to Him. He wants to bless you as much
as you want to bless your own children. It's magical to
be God's child at Christmas.

A CHRISTMAS MESSAGE

Love is like magic and it always will be,
For love still remains life's sweet mystery.
Love works in ways that are
    wondrous and strange,
And there's nothing in life
    that love cannot change.
Love can transform the most commonplace
Into beauty and splendor
    and sweetness and grace.
Love is unselfish, understanding, and kind,
For it sees with its heart and not with its mind.
Love is the answer that everyone seeks;
Love is the language that every heart speaks.
Love is the message that was sent to earth
On that first holy Christmas that
    heralded Christ's birth!

~HSR

THE SPIRIT OF
THE SEASON

*Above all, love each other deeply, because love
covers over a multitude of sins.*
1 PETER 4:8

Families aren't perfect. How could they be? No one's perfect.
But our imperfections are no surprise to God. He swaddles the
best and the worst of who we are in His wonderful, transforming
love.

God looks at us with loving eyes at Christmas and every
other day of the year, and He has given us the ability to look at
others in the same way. That "just because" kind of love is, in its
purest form, a gift. It communicates that no matter how flawed
a person might be, there is something of worth inside them.
Such love has been known to initiate miracles, change behaviors,
soften attitudes, heal wounds, adjust perspectives, and transform
lives.

Is it easy to love each member of our families? The reality is
that some individuals will pose a greater challenge than others.
Regardless of where they stand on the difficulty scale, give the
gift of love this year to everyone in your family. Look around the
room when your family is gathered together and ask God to help
you see each one through His eyes of love. You may be surprised
to discover that unconditional love contains its own reward,
blessing the giver as much as the receiver.

CELEBRATING FRIENDS

GIVE LAVISHLY!
LIVE ABUNDANTLY!

The more you give, the more you get;
The more you laugh, the less you fret;
The more you do unselfishly,
The more you live abundantly.
The more of everything you share,
The more you'll always have to spare;
The more you love, the more you'll find
That life is good and friends are kind.
For only what we give away,
Enriches us from day to day.
So let's live Christmas through the year
And fill the world with love and cheer.

~HSR

Close at Heart

*I have called you friends, for everything that I
learned from my Father I have made known to you.*
John 15:15

It has been said that friends are the family you get to choose.
What a wonderful way of looking at friendship! While we are
not connected to our friends by blood, these relationships can
be as strong as, or stronger in many cases, than traditional family
bonds. The Bible tells us that King David had such a friend—his
name was Jonathan. The two men were completely committed
to their friendship even though Jonathan's father, King Saul, had
embarked on a campaign to kill David, his political rival.

If you have friends this Christmas, hold them closely to your
heart and cherish them. Know they are gifts to you from God,
just as you are a gift from God to them. Go out of your way to let
them know how much they mean to you, how much you would
be diminished without them.

Did you know that God has called us His friends? It's true!
In addition to being our heavenly Father, He wants us to know
He also sees us as friends. What an honor that is!

This Christmas and throughout the year ahead, treat your
friends as the family you have chosen—bless them, encourage
them, appreciate them, and pour out your love on them, just as
our heavenly Father does for His friends.

LOVING FRIENDS

Among the great and glorious gifts
our heavenly Father sends
Is the gift of understanding that we find in loving friends.
For it's not money or gifts or material things,
But understanding the joy it brings,
That can change this old world in wonderful ways
And put goodness and mercy back in our days.

~HSR

The Best Gift

He who cherishes understanding prospers.
PROVERBS 19:8

*F*inding just the right gift at Christmas can be a challenge.
We think we know our friends and family: who they are, what
makes them smile, their hopes and desires—but do we? Often
we impose our own desires on those we love. Our human
understanding fails us.

God, however, never fails in His understanding. Because He
created us, He knows both our wants and our needs. He knew
we needed love and lots of it. He knew we needed fellowship.
He knew we would flounder in this cold and troubled world if
we were left alone. We would soon buckle under the weight of
our burdens and weaken in our resolve.

He knew. . .and that's why He gave us the gift of friendship.
It was a gift based on His deepest understanding of us;
one more way that He has proven He knows us inside
and out.

Ask God to help you truly understand your friends.
Forego the simple answer and the quick judgment and
try to follow God's example. Choose a gift that touches
the heart. It's bound to bring a smile.

KINDNESS IS A CIRCLE

Like roses in a garden,
  kindness fills the air
With a certain bit of sweetness
  as it touches everywhere.
For kindness is a circle
  that never, never ends
But just keeps ever-widening
  in the circle of our friends.
For the more you give, the more you get
  is proven every day,
And so to get the most from life
  you must give yourself away.

~HSR

Spreading Warmth and Cheer

Do what is right and true.
Be kind and merciful to each other.
Zechariah 7:9 NCV

When the world is harsh and unforgiving, our friends provide warmth, understanding, and kindness. They surround us with a strong defense of love and compassion. Without them, we would face every crisis alone. We see God's love for us in their encouraging words, tender gestures, and uplifting smiles—especially at Christmas.

In fact, at Christmas the entire world seems to take on the nature of friendship, if only for a brief time. The kindness we see within our circle of friends is extended even to strangers. We move into action on behalf of the poor, the sick, and the homeless. We gather gifts and write checks for those in need. We gladly donate our time and effort in order to ensure that the lives of others are enriched.

We will always appreciate those who are closest to us—those with whom we share the gift of friendship. But imagine how our world would be changed if every day were Christmas, if we were always willing to extend kindness and goodwill no matter what the season. Not only would the lives of others be changed, but our own would be as well.

Think about what you do for others during the holidays. Then imagine how good it would feel to give yourself away each day of the year.

LOYAL FRIEND

Nothing on earth can make
  life more worthwhile
Than a true, loyal friend
  and the warmth of a smile.
For, just like a sunbeam makes
  the cloudy day brighter,
The smile of a friend makes
  a heavy heart lighter.

~HSR

PRESERVING CHRISTMAS JOY

A merry heart makes a cheerful countenance.
PROVERBS 15:13 NKJV

*S*miles are a hallmark of the Christmas season. Shoppers smile as they select their gifts. Friends smile as they open cards expressing messages of love and Christmas cheer. Parents smile as they tuck their little ones into bed on Christmas Eve and pull out the gift-wrapped secrets they've been hiding. Children with cheeks glowing in anticipation open the gifts they've been dreaming about for weeks. Older members of the family smile as they sit and watch the joyful chaos. Neighbors wear smiles as they stand framed in the doorway, dropping off goodies and singing carols. Oh yes, Christmas is all about smiles.

Smiles are wonderful at Christmas, but wouldn't it be grand to have them grace our lives all year long? Perhaps it wouldn't take too much—just the warmth of human kindness, special goodnights with our little ones, and time spent listening to our elders' stories and appreciating their wise counsel. Wouldn't it be easy to choose a small, unexpected gift for a friend or family member and bring a smile to that person's face? It's not hard to make friends smile—a loving note or an encouraging call just to say, "I'm praying for you," or "I'm thinking of you," is sometimes all it takes. Couldn't we all be purveyors of Christmas smiles throughout the year?

EVERYBODY NEEDS A FRIEND

For in this world of trouble
    that is filled with anxious care,
Everybody needs a friend
    in whom they're free to share,
The little secret heartaches
    that lay heavy on their mind.
We seek a true and trusted friend
    in the knowledge that we'll find
A heart that's sympathetic
    and an understanding mind.

                              ~HSR

LETTING GENEROSITY FLOURISH

Some friends play at friendship but a true friend sticks closer than one's nearest kin.
PROVERBS 18:24 NRSV

Friendship is an expensive undertaking simply because it costs us part of ourselves. If you want to have a true friend, you must be one. You must be willing to give to another person your love, your caring, your time, your understanding, your listening ear, your best advice, your availability, and your constant loyalty. You have to learn to temper your words and be careful with someone else's feelings. You must treat that other person with the same deference you would typically reserve for yourself. And you will need to be happy when that person is happy, sad when that person is sad, and there for that person even when it isn't convenient and even when you don't feel like it.

Being a friend is, at the very least, a lot of hard work, but it pays extraordinary dividends. When you find someone who appreciates your friendship and repays it in kindness, you have found a treasure that will only grow more valuable with time. This Christmas, determine to show your appreciation by being an even better friend than you have ever been before. And remember that God has offered you His friendship. What a wonder and a privilege! Truly there has never been a better friend than the One who gave His very best when we needed it most.

LIFE'S GIFTS OF LOVE

If people like me didn't
  know people like you,
Life would lose its meaning
  and its richness, too.
For the friends that we make
  are life's gifts of love,
And I think friends are sent
  right from heaven above.
And thinking of you
  somehow makes me feel
That God is Love
  and He's very real.

~HSR

REACHING OUT

Love one another with mutual affection;
outdo one another in showing honor.
ROMANS 12:10 NRSV

Christmas is a sentimental time—a time to look back and give
thanks for our blessings—especially for those people we call
friends. We sit in front of the fireplace, soaking up the luxurious
warmth as memories of our friends' faces dance through our
minds. We recall that some were easier to forge a relationship
with than others. For one reason or another, certain friends
simply could not reach out. Perhaps they had been hurt in
some way or lacked the ability to trust. They could have had a
shy nature or a sense of unworthiness about themselves. But
no matter what their reason, we know that there are just some
people who are unable to take the first step toward friendship.
In such cases, it is necessary to risk rejection in order to
establish a relationship.

That's what God did for us on that first Christmas morning.
We could not reach out to Him, so He reached down to us. He
wrapped His holy Son Jesus in the body of a child and delivered
Him here so He could introduce Himself to us. He risked
rejection in order to establish a relationship with us. In that
sense, friendship is the essence of Christmas—love offered in
the hope of love returned.

FRIENDSHIP BLOOMS

Friendship, like flowers,
looms ever more fair
When carefully tended by
dear friends who care;
And life's lovely garden
would be sweeter by far
If all who passed through it
were as nice as you are.

~HSR

Sharing Every Season

A friend loves at all times, and a brother is born for adversity.
PROVERBS 17:17

Christmas is a wonderful time because it offers so many opportunities to tell those we love how we feel about them. We meet friends for lunch and gather for parties. We send out Christmas cards and bring goodies into the office to share. We even find time to send greetings to those who deliver our mail and our newspapers. We look for ways to bless others and acknowledge our friends.

True friends, though, are like beautiful flowers growing in a garden. They need to be gently watered and tended to all year long. Do your friends receive the care they need from you? It's easy to let those gestures of kindness and solidarity slip amid busy schedules and never-ending responsibilities. We mean to plan a get-together, drop by, or make a call, but life interferes and those things just don't get done.

If we would just resolve to cherish and nurture our friendships all year long, think how much richer those Christmas activities would be. Rather than catch-up times, they would be true celebrations infused with real-time familiarity rather than emotional memories. Your friends are one of the greatest gifts God has given you. Make sure they are well tended.

WHEN YOU ASK GOD

Gold is cold and lifeless,
    it cannot see or hear,
And in your times of trouble,
    it is powerless to cheer.
It has no ears to listen,
    no heart to understand.
It cannot bring you comfort
    or reach out a helping hand.
So when you ask God for a gift,
    be thankful that He sends,
Not diamonds, pearls, or riches,
    but the love of a real, true friend.

~HSR

True Riches

Command those who are rich in this present
world not to be arrogant nor to put their hope
in wealth, which is so uncertain, but to put their
hope in God, who richly provides us with
everything for our enjoyment.
1 Timothy 6:17

It is a fortunate person who has one true friend in a lifetime—someone who will be there in the good times and the bad times. If you have two, you are rich indeed!

We live in a world of misplaced values. Many would define "fortunate" as a big win in the lottery or some other financial windfall. The "riches" of life are counted quantitatively rather than qualitatively. Look around at those we call celebrities. We often assign them value based on the number of homes they own, how many millions of dollars they made on their last movie, or where they go on vacation. But money and possessions are shallow good fortune. They cannot bring lasting happiness or satisfaction. Quickly, the heart begins yearning for something more, something real—a human connection.

If you are a fortunate person, rich beyond imagination with the love and faithfulness of true friends, honor them from your heart this Christmas. Find the words to tell them what their friendship means to you every day of the year. And thank God for giving them to you—they are the best Christmas gifts you will ever receive!

CELEBRATING OTHERS

A SEASON OF KINDNESS

May the kindly spirit of Christmas
   spread its radiance far and wide,
So all the world may feel the glow
   of this holy Christmastide.
Then may every heart and home
   continue through the year
To feel the warmth and wonder
   of this season of good cheer.
And may it bring us closer
   to God and to each other
Till every stranger is a friend
   and every man a brother.

~HSR

REVITALIZING THE CHRISTMAS SPIRIT

He who is kind to the poor lends to the LORD,
and he will reward him for what he has done.
PROVERBS 19:17

It seems that Christmas brings out the best in all of us. Burly bikers and popular celebrities collect toys for needy children, food drives are abundant, and soup kitchens hand out baskets filled with holiday fare. Bell ringers with big red kettles urge us to donate our spare change. No one wants to think about someone going hungry or families struggling to provide for themselves during the holidays. And we know God is pleased with all this effort on behalf of others.

If you are finding that Christmas has lost its luster and excitement, leaving you feeling empty and deflated, you may want to approach this holiday season with a sacrificial attitude—putting your own wants aside and dedicating yourself to making the season merry for those less fortunate than yourself. You might also want to think about making your donation personal. In addition to food, toy, and monetary contributions to charitable organizations, perhaps you can reach out to a struggling family that you know personally. Respectfully and anonymously set out to make their holiday something special. You may find that the joy and lasting satisfaction you feel is the best Christmas gift you've ever received.

YOU!

For every day's a good day
   to lose yourself in others
And any time's a good time
   to see mankind as brothers,
And this can only happen
   when you realize it's true
That everyone needs someone
   and that someone is you!

~HSR

Take Action

*The Master said... "Turn both your
pockets and your hearts inside out
and give generously to the poor."*
LUKE 11:41 MSG

At Christmas we are more aware of the
needs of those around us, but we fail to
keep in mind that there are many who need our help throughout
the year. Jesus said that the poor will always be with us, and
their numbers are certainly growing every day. For each person
offering a helping hand, two more are still in need.

It's clear that we can't help everyone by ourselves. The
need is too great for any one person to bear. However, we can
initiate a chain of blessing by passing kindness on to others and
encouraging them to do the same. In this way, we become God's
hands and feet, giving His love momentum and force. God can
and will use whatever you give, no matter how great or how
small. In His capable hands, miracles happen. Just as He did
with the little boy's loaves and fishes, His blessings can multiply
exponentially.

It has been said that a good deed is its own reward. Try it
and you'll know it's true. When you give to others, God repays
you by fulfilling your own needs. The principle is simple: As you
reach out to help others, He reaches out to help you. That's an
investment you can bank on at Christmas and all year long.

IN GOD'S SIGHT

No one is a stranger in God's sight,
For God is love and in His light
May we, too, try in our small way
To make new friends from day to day. . .
So pass no stranger with an unseeing eye,
For God may be sending a new friend by.

~HSR

True Gifts

Do not neglect to do good and to share what you have,
for such sacrifices are pleasing to God.
HEBREWS 13:16 NRSV

When we give at Christmas, we usually think in terms of money, toys, and food—all kinds of material gifts. But the spirit of Christmas giving is much greater in scope. It is also dressed in a garment of kindness, thoughtfulness, encouragement, and sensitivity.

Material gifts are great. They bring relief during difficult times, alleviate stress, and curb worry. But material gifts are soon used up. No matter how many meals you provide for someone, at some point that person will be hungry again. However, gifts given from the heart transcend material things. Their effects are permanent.

A simple kind word or gesture can change a life forever. Including those who feel left out, caring for someone who feels unloved, listening to someone who feels unappreciated, offering friendship to a stranger—these gifts can make a lasting impression on the lives of those who receive them.

Expand your giving this year to include gifts of grace. These are not gifts you can pick up quickly at a department store. Each one is uniquely crafted for a particular person. Give generously this year.

SERVE GOD THROUGH OTHERS

Great is our gladness
   to serve God through others,
For our Father taught us
   we are all sisters and brothers,
And the people we meet
   on life's thoroughfares
Are burdened with trouble
   and sorrow and cares.
And this is the chance
   we are given each day
To witness for God,
   and to try to obey.

~HSR

The Gift that Keeps Giving

God's gift is eternal life given by Jesus Christ our Lord.
ROMANS 6:23 CEV

*O*n that very special Christmas so many years ago, God gave to mankind the greatest gift ever given. It was a gift of freedom, a gift of rescue, a gift with the potential to transform those who were hopeless and lost into people with a joyful, peace-filled future. That gift was not an "it" at all though. "It" was a "Him" with a capital H. Right there in that unassuming stable, God gave us His very own Son in the form of a tiny child—a child who would grow and mature and one day reconcile us to our Creator. This gift was an eternity in the making, so magnificent that we can comprehend it only with the help of the Holy Spirit.

A gift so grand was never meant to be stuck in the corner of our hearts and left there. Jesus was meant to be shared. We are meant to carry Him to our friends, our family, and to all those we encounter in our lives. Just as the shepherds did on that first Christmas morning, we should be praising and glorifying God so loudly that all will gather to hear His story.

LOVE LIKE HIS

Love is the answer to all the heart seeks,
And love is the channel through which God speaks——
And all He has promised can only come true
When you love one another the way He loved you.

~HSR

Spreading His Love

Keep alert, stand firm in your faith, be courageous, be strong.
Let all that you do be done in love.
1 Corinthians 16:13–14 NRSV

Mary and Joseph's long journey, the stable in Bethlehem, the birth of the Holy Child, the angel's declaration, the shepherds' visit, the gifts from the Magi—*all* of these Christmas images can be summed up with one word: love. God loved us so much that He took extraordinary measures to reconcile us to Himself. The gift of His Son demonstrated His love in the most personal way possible, and He asks us to share that love with all those we meet.

You may be thinking, "I can't tell other people about the Gift; I'm not a preacher." Don't worry. All God asks is that you spread His love through your words and actions. And if someone asks where all your love comes from, you can tell them it's all about Christmas.

You don't need to be a preacher or theologian to share God's love. You don't need to be in a church to show others how much He cares either. You don't need any "special" words, accounts of miracles, or other tools of persuasion. When you know you're truly loved, it shows in everything you say and do.

KINDNESS IS A VIRTUE

*K*indness is a virtue given by the Lord,
It pays dividends in happiness
   and joy is its reward. . .
For if you practice kindness
   in all you say and do,
The Lord will wrap His kindness
   around your heart and you.

~HSR

Good Will to All

As God's chosen ones, holy and beloved,
clothe yourselves with compassion, kindness,
humility, meekness, and patience.
COLOSSIANS 3:12 NRSV

Kindness is more than thoughtful words and actions—it is also defined as the state of being kind. It's an attitude, a way of living, a well-exercised habit. If we truly want to emulate the kindness God showed when He sent us His Son to be born in Bethlehem's manger, then we must make it a living, breathing part of who we are every day of the year.

An attitude of kindness must start from within. Do we judge others by the color of their skin? What about those from unfamiliar cultures? Can we extend kind gestures to those who do not share our opinions about politics and religion? How about those whose lifestyles we disapprove of?

It's easy to be kind to those who think like we do, look like we do, and act like we do. But it is far more difficult to show kindness to those who don't. We must remember that kindness neither condemns nor condones. It just is. God in all His holiness reached out in kindness to *all* of us, without reservation. His loving kindness is extended to every living soul. Glorify Him by asking that your own attitude of kindness would become as broad as a sky filled with angels.

CELEBRATING CHRISTMAS BLESSINGS

GIVING

Christmas is a season of giving,
And giving is the key to living.
So let us give ourselves away,
Not just at Christmas but every day,
And remember a kind and thoughtful deed,
Or a hand outstretched in a time of need
Is the rarest of gifts for it is a part
Not of the purse but a loving heart;
And he who gives of himself will find
True joy of heart and peace of mind.

~HSR

Full Circle Blessings

I will send down showers in season;
there will be showers of blessing.
EZEKIEL 34:26

*A*t Christmas, blessings come in showers as predictable as winter snowstorms. We work hard to make things merry for everyone we know by baking goodies, buying gifts, putting up beautiful decorations, and sending out Christmas cards. We are preoccupied with blessing others—so much so that we literally get caught up in the joy and excitement of doing things for others rather than for ourselves.

Christmas gives us the opportunity to learn the truth about blessings: The more you bless others, the more you yourself are blessed. It's as though we are engaged in an experiment of global proportions. We reach out with blessings to one person and soon someone else is blessing us, until finally showers of blessing are pouring from one person to another in earnest.

The interesting thing is that some people practice blessing others all year long. They carry soup to sick friends, give a hand whenever and wherever they can, babysit for an overloaded mom, or pay an encouraging visit to someone who is lonely. They are always on the lookout for ways to bless others. And they have learned that those blessings will return—maybe not in the form of chicken soup or babysitting, but in a way that will meet their needs. Imagine, refreshing showers of blessings even on the hottest summer day!

IT FILLS ME WITH JOY

It fills me with joy just to linger with You,
As my soul You replenish and my heart You renew.
So thank You again for Your mercy and love
And for making me heir to Your kingdom above.

~HSR

GLAD TIDINGS

God once said, "Let the light shine out of the darkness!"
This is the same God who made his light shine in our hearts by
letting us know the glory of God that is in the face of Christ.
2 CORINTHIANS 4:6 NCV

The angel spoke of "tidings of great joy that would be to all people." Then he announced to the shepherds that the Messiah had been born. Can you imagine what the shepherds made of that? Would the arrival of the Messiah change their lives? Would their Roman oppressors be overthrown? What would life under a new king be like?

How could they know that the birth of Christ was not about politics or bringing equity between the rich and the poor? His mission was far more important than that. His work was and is in the hearts and minds of men and women. That's where He intended to pour out His blessings and deliver tidings of great joy—one human heart at a time.

The message of Christ's birth transcends national boundaries and political hierarchies. The Child who lay in Bethlehem's manger was intended to bless you, inside and out; to give you a new lease on life and open the gates of heaven to you. He was intended to bring you peace and joy and eternal fellowship with your Creator. He was intended to bless you with a bright future.

HUSHED MEDITATION

*B*righten your day
And lighten your way
And lessen your cares
With daily prayers.
Quiet your mind
And leave tension behind
And find inspiration
In hushed meditation.

~HSR

Escaping the Hustle and Bustle

In quietness and confidence
shall be your strength.
ISAIAH 30:15 NKJV

It's not an easy thing to find a quiet moment during the holidays. With shopping, baking, decorating, and entertaining, it all seems to go by in a blur. It could be said, however, that making time for quiet meditation is more necessary during the holidays than at any other time of year. Unless we do, it's possible that we'll miss some of God's most joyful blessings.

Christmas has great meaning to all of Christendom and even to the secular world. As the angels said, the season's good tidings were meant for all. First and foremost though, Christmas is about the individual heart reconnecting with God's heart. The Christ Child came on behalf of *all* of us and just as certainly for *each* of us. It's possible to be part of the shared blessing that comes from being with family and friends and reaching out to others and still miss out on the personal blessing that comes from spending time quietly resting alone in His presence.

As you schedule your activities during the Christmas season, set aside some time each week—or even each day—to spend with your heavenly Father. It's an investment that will give the holidays new meaning and a true sense of joy.

COUNTING YOUR BLESSINGS

*H*appiness is something we create
  in our minds—
It's not something you search for
  and so seldom find.
It's just waking up and beginning the day
By counting our blessings
  and kneeling to pray.

~HSR

What Matters Most

May the Lord bless you from Zion all the days of your life.
Psalm 128:5

Some people would tell you they don't enjoy the holidays. Christmas has lost its charm, and they are certain they know why. No matter how they approach the season, they quickly find themselves feeling overwhelmed—as though Christmas were in charge and they are just being dragged along behind.

The next year they determine to start sooner and plan better in order to stay in control, but something always comes along that they don't anticipate. Maybe one year they put some money aside each month to prepare a Christmas budget, only to get hit with an unexpected expense that puts them right back where they started. Or they might start their shopping early, only to encounter an illness or other circumstance that leaves them once again doing last-minute shopping. The frustration takes the fun right out of the season.

If you've become one of those bah-humbug people, perhaps it's time to encourage yourself with these thoughts. The blessing is not in pulling off a perfect Christmas with each bow in place. Nor is it in how much you spend or how lavishly you decorate. The blessing in Christmas is waking up and realizing how deeply and eternally you are loved by your Creator.

IN HIS CARE

God is no stranger in a faraway place—
He's as close as the wind that blows 'cross my face.
It's true I can't see the wind as it blows,
But I feel it around me, and my heart surely knows
That God's mighty hand can be felt everywhere,
For there's nothing on earth that is not in God's care.

~HSR

So Many Ways to Celebrate

When I look at your heavens, the work of your fingers, the moon and the stars that you have established; what are human beings that you are mindful of them, mortals that you care for them? Yet you have made them a little lower than God, and crowned them with glory and honor.
PSALM 8:3–5 NRSV

One of the great and wonderful aspects of Christmas is that it is celebrated in countless nations with a vast variety of customs and traditions. For example, the French celebrate *Joyeux Noel* with a gift exchange on December 6. Belgians celebrate *Zalige Kertfeest*, and believe that on Christmas Day animals talk to each other about the birth of Christ. In Poland, *Boze Narodzenie* is celebrated, which includes a twenty-four-hour fast lasting until the first star can be seen and followed by a huge twelve-course feast.

In homes around the world, Christmas is a time of joy, a time to remember the Christ Child in the manger. God is watching over each celebration, and His hand of blessing reaches out to each person.

You may be far from home this Christmas, wondering what that very special day will be like in unfamiliar surroundings. But no matter where you find yourself, you can be certain God is there, watching over you. Whether you join in with those in whose company you find yourself or quietly celebrate in your own time-tested way, you needn't worry. Look up and you will see the remnants of that Christmas star embedded in the sky above and joyful hearts all around.

A CHRISTMAS
PRAYER OF BLESSING

Our Father, who art in heaven,
    hear this Christmas prayer,
And if it be Thy gracious will,
    may joy be everywhere—
The joy that comes from knowing
    that the holy Christ Child came
To bless the earth at Christmas
    for Thy sake and in Thy name.
And with this prayer there comes a wish,
    that these holy, happy days
Will bless your loved ones everywhere
    in many joyous ways.

~HSR

THE MOST JOYFUL NIGHT

*The grace of God that brings salvation
has appeared to all men.*
TITUS 2:11

From the time of Adam and Eve, God-fearing people have lived
in anticipation of the one seminal event that would repair the
breach between God and man. The Old Testament speaks of it
again and again, sometimes in the simplest common language and
sometimes in veiled prophetic speech. That event can be found
in each and every book of the Old Testament and is indeed the
common denominator that pulls them all together.

The Old Testament promises what the New Testament
reports: God in His tender mercy and loving-kindness refused
to live without us forever. He found a way, a way so unique and
personal that we can barely comprehend it. Angels and shepherds
watched as it played out on a simple starlit stage as humble
travelers, shepherds, wise men from afar, and the host of heaven
looked on. That event was the birth of our Immanuel, meaning
God with us. The holy child would soon purchase our salvation.

It's no surprise that the angels were filled with joy on that
blessed night. They must have been waiting for millennia to
hear their announcement echo through the countryside. Even
as we read about it now, our hearts are blessed with joy and
thankfulness at the thought of God's faithfulness and love.

IT'S ALL GOD. . .

Each time you look up in the sky
Or watch the fluffy clouds drift by,
Or feel the sunshine warm and bright,
Or watch the dark night turn to light,
Or hear a bluebird sweetly sing,
Or see the winter turn to spring,
Or touch a leaf or see a tree,
It's all God whispering, "This is Me. . ."

~HSR

Making the Season Last

*T*here is great excitement on Christmas night as we all gather to remember the birth of Christ. The air seems charged with anticipation as we prepare to celebrate the great story of the Christ Child and His mission to bless all of mankind with the joy of salvation. It's a special time. And it should be a time that we want to carry with us and cherish throughout the year.

On almost any night of the year, barring clouds and the city lights, it's possible to look up into the sky and remember that it was one amazing star that led the Magi to Mary and Joseph and their infant Son. On any day, it is possible to experience the joy and peace of knowing we are no longer estranged from our Creator but happily incorporated into His family and even called sons and daughters. At any time, it is possible to share that joy with others, give from the heart with gratitude, and reach out with an attitude of acceptance and goodwill to those around us.

Let every day be a day of Christmas blessing in your heart. No need to wait until Christmas carols replace the top ten on the radio or holiday movie specials grace the television screen. Bless yourself and others with Christmas every day.

TRUE HAPPINESS

You need nothing more than God's guidance and love
To ensure the things that you're most worthy of. . .
So trust in His wisdom and follow His ways,
And be not concerned with the world's empty praise,
But seek first His kingdom, and you will possess
The world's greatest riches, which is true happiness.

~HSR

Glorious Realization

May the righteous be glad and rejoice before God;
may they be happy and joyful.
Psalm 68:3

Have you ever felt so happy that you couldn't resist bursting into song and dancing a little jig? Wonderful, isn't it! We'd all love to feel that way all the time. That must have been how the shepherds felt when the heavenly host appeared in the sky above them with their glad tidings of great joy. Once they realized the friendly nature of their visitation, they must have been quite beside themselves. Imagine being singled out to receive the angelic announcement of God's ultimate plan for the reconciliation of all mankind to the great Creator.

But for the shepherds, there must have also been the quiet happiness that came later as they reflected on what they had been given; the great blessing that was now theirs.

You may remember the moment the gravity of it all first struck you, the first time you realized that God loved you so much that He reached down from heaven to initiate your rescue and pour out His blessings on you. Now that's singing and dancing news! But later, you experienced a constant inner happiness that sprang from the realization that you had been given such a marvelous gift. The Bible says that Mary pondered those things in her heart, and you undoubtedly will, too.

IT'S A WONDERFUL WORLD

A warm, ready smile or a kind,
    thoughtful deed
Or a hand outstretched in an hour of need
Can change our whole outlook
    and make the world bright
Where a minute before
    just nothing seemed right—
It's a wonderful world and it always will be
If we keep our eyes open and focused to see
The wonderful things man is capable of
When he opens his heart to God and His love.

~HSR

SPREAD THE NEWS!

See if I will not open the windows
of heaven for you and pour down
for you an overflowing blessing.
MALACHI 3:10 NRSV

*A*s you celebrate Christmas, give some
thought to the fact that all we have today emanates from the
events of that cold night in that lowly stable. Hearts filled with
hope and promise, freedom from the mistakes of the past, the
love of family and friends—all that and so very much more is
ours because that little babe who lay in that manger bed grew up
and became the Savior of the world. In fact, through Jesus, all the
blessings of God are available to each one of us.

We should also remember that blessings, like love and
kindness, were never meant to be held tightly to the chest. They
were meant to be shared. In fact, when they are shared, they
quickly multiply and leave the person who blesses others with
even more blessings for himself.

God shared with us the blessing of His Son, fully expecting
that we would share Him with others just as freely and
abundantly. Ask God to help you realize the height, depth, and
breadth of His goodness to you, the real riches of His grace.
Then as you awaken to the blessings around you, pass them on to
everyone who crosses your path.

CELEBRATING THE REASON FOR THE SEASON

THE CHRIST CHILD'S BIRTH

In our Christmas celebrations
   of merriment and mirth,
Let us not forget the miracle
   of the holy Christ Child's birth.
For in our festivities
   it is easy to lose sight
Of the baby in the manger
   and that holy, silent night.

~HSR

CHRISTMAS MIRACLE

Glory to God in the highest,
and on earth peace, goodwill toward men!
LUKE 2:14 NKJV

*H*as there ever been a birth more celebrated than that of the Christ Child? Almost every culture has a version of the story, which includes the elements listed in the Bible—shepherds, angels, Magi, Mary and Joseph, taxation, a Roman emperor named Herod, a donkey, a stable, farm animals, a manger, and an inn with no room. This is a story that transcends borders and languages. It is a story that belongs to the whole world.

When God sent His Son to dwell among us, He did not send Him strictly on behalf of Americans or Australians or Africans. The mission of the Christ Child included every human being, without exception or prejudice. He lived and died for us all! Not only was His birth a miracle, but He opened for us a higher realm—the realm of miracles.

That baby wrapped in swaddling clothes and lying in a manger was much more than just a symbol or an icon to be worshipped. He was a real person who grew and matured and gave His life for you—personally. Reach out and claim your miracle this Christmas, the miracle of a life transformed.

THIS IS THE SAVIOR OF THE WORLD

Some regard the Christmas story
as something beautiful to hear,
A lovely Christmas custom
that we celebrate each year.
But it's more than just a story
told to make our hearts rejoice;
It's our Father up in heaven
speaking through the Christ Child's voice,
Telling us of heavenly kingdoms
that He has prepared above
For those who put their trust
in His mercy and His love.
And only through the Christ Child
can man be born again,
For God sent the baby Jesus
as the Savior of all men.

~HSR

LET HIS LOVE IN

God so loved the world that he gave his one and only Son, that whoever believes in him shall not perish but have eternal life.
JOHN 3:16

*P*eace and joy are intricately woven into the Christmas story; but love—that's what it's all about. God loved us, His grandest creation, even though we had become quite unlovely. He entrusted us with a free will, and we used it to muddy ourselves, separating us from His glory and perfection. He could have thrown us away and begun fresh, but He didn't. Instead He initiated His plan to redeem us, a plan that began with the birth of a very special child. That child, part God and part man, would willingly pay the price for our errant behavior. He would bring us back to our Father.

Yes, we have been touched by God's love and cleansed by it. And for that reason, we can now love and be loved not only at Christmas but every day of the year! If that seems overwhelming to comprehend, begin by simply receiving the love God has for you. He's taken care of everything, and now He's there waiting, longing to have you back in His arms where you belong. Won't you let Him show you what true love is all about? Once you know, you can share it with others, and shared love is a beautiful thing.

CHRISTMAS GLITTER

With our eyes
    we see the glitter of Christmas,
With our ears
    we hear the merriment,
With our hands
    we touch the tinsel-tied trinkets,
But only with our hearts
    can we feel the miracle of it.

~HSR

BLESSED REMINDERS

Suddenly there was with the angel a multitude
of the heavenly host praising God.
LUKE 2:13 NKJV

*F*or most of us, Christmas would not
be Christmas without certain familiar trappings—the tree, the
ornaments, the angel at the top, the holly, the candles, and the
candy canes. We take them for granted because they have always
been part of our Christmas tradition. But it turns out that each
one has a special significance related to the true meaning of
Christmas.

The tree, traditionally an evergreen, symbolizes the eternal
nature of God and urges us to remember that His presence in our
lives is always fresh and alive. The ornaments, which in olden
times were fruits and nuts, represent the way God abundantly
provides for us. The angel at the top of the tree represents the
glorious nature of the celestial announcement of Christ's birth.
The holly leaves point to the crown of thorns that Christ wore
at His crucifixion—the berries represent His blood and the
evergreen color represents eternal life. The candles remind
us that Jesus lights the world with hope. And the candy cane,
though its true origins are not known, has come to symbolize
Jesus, by simultaneously representing the letter *J* and a shepherd's
crook. The traditional red and white coloring is also reminiscent
of His purity and shed blood. Take time this Christmas to look at
these precious symbols with new insight.

SILENT NIGHT, HOLY NIGHT

Let us listen in silence so we may hear
The Christmas message more clearly this year.
Silently the green leaves grow;
In silence falls the soft, white snow.
Silently the flowers bloom;
In silence sunshine fills a room.
Silently bright stars appear;
In silence velvet night draws near.
And silently God enters in
To free a troubled heart from sin,
For God works silently in lives,
And nothing spiritual survives
Amid the din of a noisy street
Where raucous crowds with hurrying feet
And blinded eyes and deafened ears
Are never privileged to hear
The message God wants to impart
To every troubled, weary heart.
So let not our worldly celebrations
Disturb our Christmas meditations,
For only in a quiet place
Can we behold God face-to-face.

~HSR

Embracing Silence

For God alone my soul waits in silence; from him comes my salvation.
He alone is my rock and my salvation, my fortress; I shall never be shaken.
Psalm 62:1–2 nrsv

With boisterous family gatherings, the radio blasting out a revolving play list of carols and seasonal songs, a constant stream of parties and yuletide activities, and shopping trips to jam-packed malls, there isn't much silence to speak of during the holidays. Only the beautiful carol "Silent Night" reminds us that there is a quiet, holy aspect to the season.

But imagine what it must have been like in that stable on that most holy of nights. Joseph, exhausted after leading the donkey carrying his wife and her unborn child over rough roads for countless miles, might have sat down to quietly keep watch over Mary and her newborn child. Perhaps, having now found a shelter from the elements and a safe place for Mary to give birth, he could finally rest.

Mary, jostled for days on the back of a donkey in her last days of pregnancy, must also have relished the silence. The arduous trip had given way to labor and delivery. Maybe now she could finally find rest.

When you feel weary and overwhelmed this Christmas, find a place where silence reigns and rest in the presence of your heavenly Father. Let His angels watch over you as He restores your strength.

KEEP CHRIST IN CHRISTMAS

If we keep Christ in Christmas
He will keep us every day,
And when we are in His keeping
and we follow in His way,
All our little earthly sorrows,
all our worries, and our cares
Seem lifted from our shoulders
when we go to God in prayer.

~HSR

Faith through Adversity

*I consider that our present sufferings are not worth
comparing with the glory that will be revealed in us.*
ROMANS 8:18

*M*ary and Joseph were both persons of great faith. The Bible
says that Joseph was a righteous man and Mary was visited by
an angel who told her she was "highly favored" and the Lord was
with her. They knew there was something wholly extraordinary
about their Son and His birth. They knew, and yet. . .they did not
hold back.

These two extraordinary people must have suffered greatly
in order to do as God asked—the accusing eyes of those who
did not know the truth, the rigors of a long journey, the plight
of giving birth in a faraway place without encouragement or
assistance or a clean room with a bed. And yet, they found room
in their hearts for wonder and praise and joyfulness. They
knew they were part of God's master plan.

Our troubles somehow seem more pronounced at
Christmas. Our worries often launch into hyperdrive.
When this happens, we must follow the example of
Mary and Joseph. Ask God to give you the same grace
and strength and courage that accompanied them on
that first Christmas night. Lift your prayers to Him
and open your heart to the wonder, praise, and joyfulness
of knowing that you, too, are part of God's plan.

THE PRESENCE OF JESUS

*J*esus came into this world
   one glorious Christmas Eve.
He came to live right here on earth
   to help us all believe.
For God up in His heaven
   knew His children all would feel
That if Jesus lived among them
   they would know that He was real
And not a far-off stranger
   who dwelt up in the sky
And knew neither joys nor sorrows
   that make us laugh and cry.
And so He walked among us
   and taught us how to love
And promised us that someday
   we would dwell with Him above.
And while we cannot see Him
   as they did, face-to-face,
We know that He is everywhere,
   and not in some far-off place.

~HSR

With Us Always

They heard the sound of the LORD God walking in
the garden in the cool of the day.
GENESIS 3:8 NKJV

Right after God created Adam and Eve,
the first people on Earth, the Bible says
God spent time walking with Adam in the cool of the day in the
beautiful garden created just for them. But a beguiler was lurking
nearby, and God had generously given His beloved people the
ability to be beguiled—the ability to choose for themselves.
Soon, there was a deception, a poor choice, a betrayal, and then a
separation. Adam and Eve left the garden.

We too have been beguiled and are separated from our
Creator. But God loved us all—from Adam and Eve on down the
line—too much to abandon us to our own willfulness. He made a
way, a bridge over troubled water, and sent us a Savior in the form
of a tiny, helpless baby.

At Christmas we remember that God returned to us in the
cool of a winter's evening as a tiny infant. As an adult, He walked
through the countryside telling us about our heavenly Father's
love. Then He walked all the way to Calvary, where He chose to
give Himself in atonement for our poor choices and reconcile us
to our Creator. Hallelujah! What a Savior!

WHAT CHRISTMAS MEANS TO ME

Christmas is more than getting and giving;
It's the why and the wherefore of infinite living.
It's the positive proof for doubting God never,
For in His kingdom, life is forever.
And this is the reason that on Christmas Day
I can only kneel and prayerfully say,
"Thank You, God, for sending Your Son
So that when my work on earth is done,
I can look at last on Your holy face,
Knowing You saved me alone by Your grace."

~HSR

Receiving True Fulfillment

Ye are all the children of God by faith in Christ Jesus.
GALATIANS 3:26 KJV

The miracle of Christmas was enacted on the human stage, but it did not originate there. It was a plan formed in heaven before the Earth began. It was a plan that lay dormant until Jesus, who was seated at the right hand of His Father, stood up and, in total submission to His Father's wishes, took on the form of an infant and was born into this world as a human being.

After living a flawless life and dying a sacrificial death, Jesus returned to His Father victorious and with the promise of many other sons and daughters yet to arrive. As each one of us takes hold of God's plan, we also become Christmas miracles. We had no hope, but now there is hope. We had no joy, but now there is joy. We had no peace, but now there is peace. We were sullied by sin, but now we are forgiven—holy children of a holy God.

Christmas was conceived in the heart of our loving Father God. It began in heaven, and it will have its greatest fulfillment there as well when each of us stands before God's throne and lays our gifts of praise at His feet.

MAY YOU FEEL THE QUIET BEAUTY

May you feel the quiet beauty
    of that holy, silent night
When God sent the little Christ Child
    to be this dark world's light.
May you know the peace He promised,
    may you feel His presence near,
Not only just at Christmas,
    but throughout a happy year.

~HSR

*Heavenly Father, You are the author of Christmas,
and on this very special day, we lift our hearts in praise
and adoration to You. We thank You for the Baby Jesus,
who grew up to become our Savior and Lord.
We thank You for the gift of Your grace. Amen.*